ANN M. MAID

SYMBOLISM
AND THE
TAROT

Everyone's Guide to Interpreting How the Universe Communicates Through the Language of Symbolism

iUniverse books may be ordered through booksellers or by contacting:

iUniverse
1663 Liberty Drive
Bloomington, IN 47403
www.iuniverse.com
1-800-Authors (1-800-288-4677)

Because of the dynamic nature of the Internet, any web addresses or links contained in this book may have changed since publication and may no longer be valid. The views expressed in this work are solely those of the author and do not necessarily reflect the views of the publisher, and the publisher hereby disclaims any responsibility for them.

Any people depicted in stock imagery provided by Getty Images are models, and such images are being used for illustrative purposes only. Certain stock imagery © Getty Images.

ISBN: 978-1-5320-7360-1 (sc)
ISBN: 978-1-5320-7361-8 (e)

Library of Congress Control Number: 2019906288

Print information available on the last page.

iUniverse rev. date: 06/05/2019

**The Major and Minor Arcana
Workbook
With
Ann M. Maid**

*Former Director and Founder of
The Village Gate Psychic Center, NY
and
The Psychic And Metaphysical Center Of Rochester,*
now known as *The Psychic Caravan, NY*
and
The Gifts of The Spirit. NC

Welcome to Tarot and the Major Arcana

… If you have this workbook, then you have an interest in learning about tarot for your own purposes or possibly for commercial use in Psychic Fairs or Reading at New Age Shoppes – whatever your reason, this workbook was designed to allow you to get the most out of your Tarot deck. You do not need to follow along the already-written text in this workbook—rather, it is important to interact with your personal deck of cards—the information in the workbook will be useful later, or when you are at home, practicing. There is a section for "NOTES" – write in there what you feel is important for you to remember; there is a section for each of the MAJOR ARCANA cards—that's where you write interpretations that you create or learn about a specific card in your Tarot deck…and also what interpretations the author shares pertaining to that card, as it resonates personally with you.

Limited number of openings on the Psychic Caravan

For Tarot Readers and palmists. If you are available to travel overnight and are interested in working as a Tarot Reader, or Palmist, please e-mail Ann Maid at a_maid55@yahoo.com

Hotels and some travel expenses, are provided for Psychic Entertainers at College and Corporate Events; Send your contact information, fields of expertise and years of experience to: a_maid55@ yahoo.com or check out our updated Website: psychic-caravan.vpweb.com and use the Contact Us Form on page 1.

The Major Arcana

0. The Fool- Naieve Innocence in risk-taking; feeling indestructible. Self-confidant.

   Reverse: Conservative, non-risk-taking, insecure, hesitant.

1. The Magician -an ambitious, intelligent, powerful and persuasive man with a lot of internal strengths; assertive, financially oriented, sensitive if needed to achieve a goal.

   Reverse: A man who abuses his position/ his power. A deceiver.

2. The High Priestess - A woman who is trusted and trustworthy; proud-intelligent; Dynamic and Assertive. Can appear cold or insensitive—very responsible and ethical.

   Reverse: A dangerous woman, self-centered—or one who is not living up to her abilities and true potential.

3. The Empress - Pregnancy or a nurturing, protective, and caring woman, creative...

   Reverse: Difficulty in pregnancy; loss of creative energy- feeling held back.

4. The Emperor – Mature man; good in business – who has acquired many things in the physical world and who has reached a position in life where he is comfortable. Admired and respected.

   Reverse: Mid- life crisis in a man; or a man who has just lost everything, possibly through divorce or financial misfortune. He feels alone and devastated.

5. The Hierophant – A High Holy card/a blessing and/or sign of being protected by a higher power. A counselor or mentor who is available for good, unbiased advice or moral support.

   Reverse: A warning to rethink your position—that you may be in a no-win situation and turning back or letting go may be a better choice

6. The Lovers – Compatibility between two people at a highest levels: mental, physical and spiritual—the complete package.

   Reverse: Two people who are breaking up or whose relationship is rocky.

7. The Chariot – Harmony, balance, peace—regaining control over our own lives.

   Reverse: Chaos – a life in turmoil, out of the control of the client.

8. Strength – Good physical health; the ability to endure and be patient through tough times; having the Courage to take a stand and make a positive difference.

   Reverse: Loss of strength and patience. Time to pull back and regroup your energies.

9. The Hermit – Higher education/knowledge/learning - - either searching for, or giving to others. Preferring solitude and study rather than engaging in the dramas of everyday Life.

   Reverse: Failure to complete education goals. The desire to be alone. Feeling unworthy.

10. Wheel of Fortune – Each person's position on the wheel of personal Progress – Being headed in the right direction or the direction which will give you opportunities for personal growth and success. The goal is to know where you are on the wheel and move along accordingly.

    Reverse: Being headed in a downward direction, or toward lessons learned the hard way. Being held back or led astray by others. Time to pay more attention to our priorities.

11. Justice – Fairness in Life. A legal matter that will be resolved in your favor.

    Reverse: Legal matter going against you… read all contracts carefully. An unfair or unjust legal situation.

12. The Sacrifice – putting the interests of others ahead of oneself. The "Christ" card. Most often it is a woman who pulls this card, and it represents herself—often sacrificing herself to put others' interests ahead of her own.

    Reverse: Turning inward to seek one's own goals. Time for putting oneself first.

13. Death – Change, transformation, transition in lifestyle and perspective.

    Reverse: Stagnation – no growth; no hope of change.

14. Temperance – Patience, Acceptance and toleration of others' shortcomings.

    Reverse: - Impatience, intolerance, haste in words. Feeling unreasonable and irritable.

15. The Devil – Our ties to the physical world; temptations to go against what we feel to be "right" action or correct behavior. Attraction without caring; lust, envy. jealousy, unethical temptations.

    Reverse: Being tempted but not giving into that temptation; steadfastly moral.

16. The Tower – The path you've been following comes abruptly to an end - - you must choose another direction. The end of a life lesson; an abrupt interruption in our lives, just when we are the most comfortable or complacent. Meant to propel us back into the Life Game when we've been spectators instead of participators for what the Universe deems is too long a time.

    Reverse: The path you're on is the one that is working for you; continue with a period of time in well-deserved peace and harmony. A reward for staying on the right path.

17. The Star – Optimistic outlook; finally being put in the spotlight to shine (a work situation) recognition by others; good fortune; a windfall; appreciation of your efforts (by others) self-awareness and fortitude in pursuit of dreams.

    Reverse: Limitations; being held back by other people's lack of knowledge, understanding or awareness of your value.

18. The Moon – Fear of the unknown; mysteries ahead; self-doubts.

    Reverse: Courage to face and/or overcome the unknown obstacles ahead.

19. The Sun – New beginnings; new ideas being put into motion; voluntary positive changes coming—initiated by oneself/client.

> Reverse: No changes; Acceptance of a life without seeking adventure; the choice of stability and predictability in lieu of risk-taking.

20. Judgement – Decision in one's favor; repentance/forgiveness; rebirth and improvement...a new lifestyle ahead, good time for needed changes.

> Reverse: Divorce/theft/procrastination or disappointment.

21. The World – Completion; fulfillment; Higher evolution...the last major transition. Unlimited opportunities still ahead—even later in life.

> Reverse: Failure to achieve- - being vulnerable, feeling unable to control external forces (environmental/physical/spiritual). Feeling helpless; withdrawing from all challenges.

Below is a space for you to write your own thoughts, AND, very importantly, add any and all meanings and interpretations <u>YOU PERSONALLY</u> find--derived from the symbolism that are valid to you *as you look at each of the images on the corresponding cards*, for now—only in the *Major Arcana*.

Notes on the Fool (#0):_____

_____

_____

_____

Notes on the Magician(#1) : _____

_____

_____

_____

Notes on the High Priestess: (#2) _____

_____

_____

_____

Notes on the the Empress: (#3) _____

_____

_____

_____

Notes on the Emperor: (#4) _____

_____

_____

_____

Notes on the Hierophant:_ (#5) _____

_____

_____

_____

Notes on the Lovers: (#6) _____

_____

_____

_____

Notes on the Chariot: (#7) _____

_____

_____

_____

Notes on Strength: (#8) _____

_____

_____

_____

Notes on the Hermit: (#9) _____

_____

_____

_____

Notes on the Wheel of Fortune (#10) _____

_____

_____

_____

Notes on Justice: (#11) _____

_____

_____

_____

Notes on Sacrifice (#12) _____

_____

_____

_____

Notes on Death: (#13) _____

_____

_____

_____

Notes on Temperance: (#14) _____

_____

_____

_____

Notes on the Devil: (#15) _____

_____

_____

_____

Notes on the Tower: (#16) _____

_____

_____

_____

Notes on the Star: (#17) _____

_____

_____

_____

Notes on the Moon: (#18) _____

_____

_____

_____

Notes on the Sun: (#19) _____

_____

_____

_____

Notes on Judgement: (#20) _____

_____

_____

_____

Notes on the World: (#21) _____

_____

_____

_____

The Celtic Cross Layout – One Year Reading (Past-Present-Future)

First Card   **Significator** Your Client – present character, assets and liabilities

2nd Card   This card *crosses* the Significator – what is immediately ahead (days/weeks)

3rd Card   This card *is "beneath" one* Foundation of the present matter or difficulty.

4th Card   This is *"behind"* one (the past)

5th Card   This is *above* one (the near future 4-8 weeks)

6th Card   This is *before/ahead of one* (near future—can be paired with Card #5)

7th Card   This is **Immediate PRESENT. Oneself** - a week past, a week to come.

8th Card   This is *family, friends, social or work environment* (Present time frame)

9th Card   *Hopes and fears* (read both in positive and negative interpretations, as neither represents current reality—only wishes and worries).

10th Card   *Far future* (within one year period of time) Culmination of growth, learning experiences and consequences of prior decisions and actions.

Final Outcomes (8-12 month time frame.)

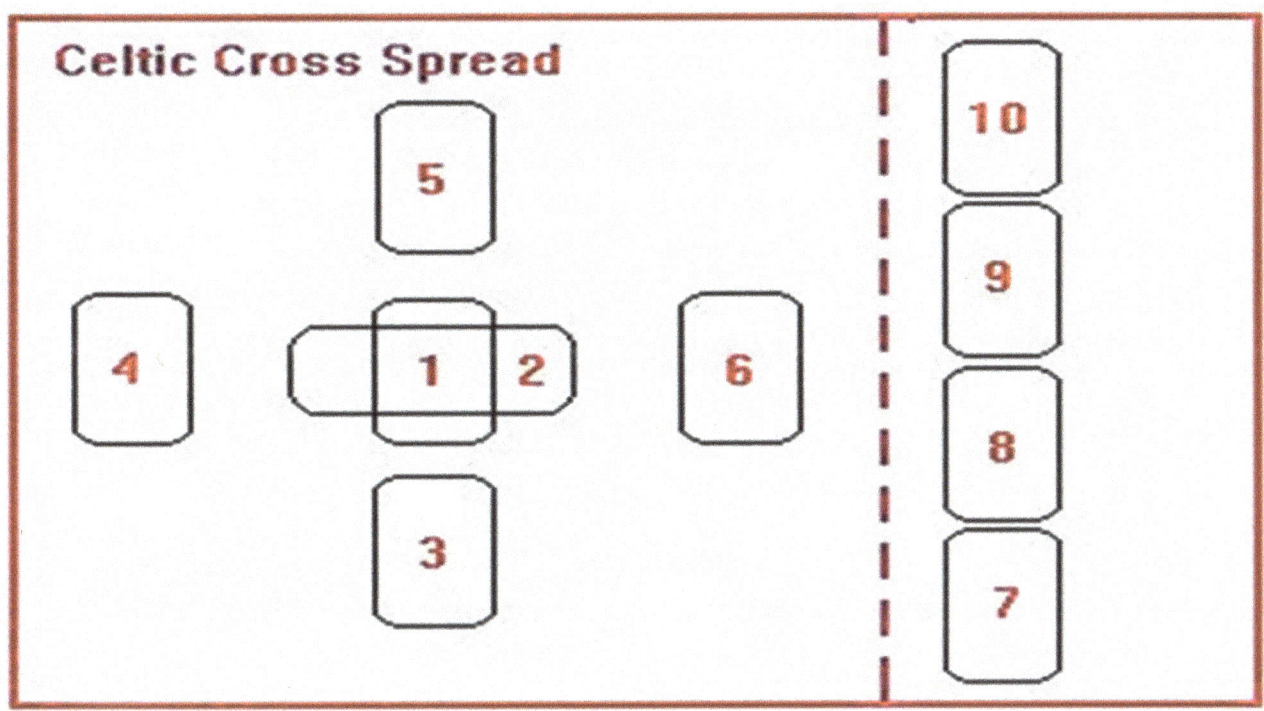

- **First Card:** *The Past* —what is important about the information contained in the card representing the past. What does it want your client to know, or remember?

- **Second Card:** *The Present* – What is your client's progress at this time in their life? What is the card saying about the client's choices or prospects in the present?

- **Third Card:** *The Future* - What's ahead for the client based on a combination of the Past information, the Present situations/assets or liabilities - - **these first two cards lead to a Future *LOGICAL progression*** of successes/ failure/growth possibilities.

1st Card: **The Fool** – represents a time in the client's Past when they were younger, full of energy and enthusiasm for whatever Adventure lay ahead; and they knew, no matter what, that they were equal to the task, win—lose--or draw—they were willing to take a risk, and face any consequences, responsibly. They were not cautious—but self-confident.

2nd Card: **The Sacrifice** – The client finds his/her path has led them to put others' needs ahead of their own—not always with positive results for the client—sometimes feeling alone or abandoned or unappreciated by the very ones he/she has tried to help.

3rd Card: **The Tower**—This may represent the future for the Client--"the path one is on comes abruptly to an end—one must choose another path". The client has gone from young, carefree risk-taking, to investing in the human condition at his/her own expense, sacrificing everything—only to find that if he/she continues on that path, it may lead to disappointment, disillusionment and personal disaster—it may be our own arrogance allowing us to think we can stand in the way of another's karmic destiny.

The Major Arcana as a Progression Through Life With Transitions of Mental & Spiritual Evolution

The **FOOL** represents the desire for knowledge and adventure and a brief time of innocence - - a time of natural protection from the outside world - -where you feel invincible and immortal. This is our youthful enthusiasm toward Life (presumably before reality sets in). It is a time of optimism. This is how we ALL start out.

Remember TAROT is composed of UNIVERSAL concepts - - applicable to every conceivable HUMAN life step.

From the risks and the initial successes we take as the **Fool** represents, we become, if we are male, **MAGICIANS**; if we are female, **The HIGH PRIESTESSES** – totally in tune for a time with Life - - the feelings of empowerment that comes with experiencing personal and/or business/career successes is embodied in these two cards. Ultimately this view of ourselves will change as a result of others' input or influences in our lives; and as a result of all the variables of Life itself - - those who can maintain the vitality and self-esteem and passion for life that these two cards represent (for both male and female), are rare indeed - - but it is interesting that in Tarot, we are never changing our roles (from a Right-Side-Up High Priestess to a reverse one - - from a Right-Side-Up Magician, to a reverse Magician… etc.)

The **EMPRESS** and the **EMPEROR**, represent Family and the influence of our parents as mature and older versions of the powerful young **Magician** and **High Priestess; The Empress** is the Eternal motherhood depiction - - nurturing, creative. Mother Earth-like; caring and protective in her role. The **Emperor** (father or male authority figure), is passive, having already attained a position of dignity in life and no longer feeling as if he must prove himself to others. He and the **Empress** together provide the highest example of the traditional family – The **Emperor** Provider; the **Empress,** nurturing mother. The ideal older, mature and stable, couple.

The **HIEROPHANT** – represents religious authority/moral influences in our life and reflects the spiritual beliefs we are given initially in the environmental, traditional value system we grew up with.

The **LOVERS** - … Now, if we are on course with the Divine Plan or the "correct" path leading to a fruitful physical and spiritual life, we start out with Innocence, a respect for ourselves (Cards 1 and 2) and what we can achieve; we have the right parents, ideally, **Emperor** and **Empress,** noble, dignified and nurturing; and we have a religious faith of some sort with which we identify as our guideline to our spiritual salvation- - what more do we need? A mate. A partner who is evenly/equally matched to us in every way: mental, spiritual and of course, physical. The **Lovers** card represents total, multi-level union, a joining of the mental, spiritual and physical natures of two people. It represents a blending of the male and female energies to create a lasting bond - - sometimes "karmic" in nature.

Well, we are attracted to someone, we bond with them, our "first" love is usually the deepest commitment we ever make, and then...

The **CHARIOT**- - for a time our lives are completely in balance and harmony. If we are female, we allow and accept that the male energy needs to be in charge; to be somewhat dominant, and we want the traditional package we are taught to expect, so our male mates "take over" their portion of the relationship is to work, provide and find solutions to problems that may come up- - however...

STRENGTH - ...as women are aware, behind every great charioteer, there is a woman encouraging him to greatness or motivating him to achieve. In most Tarot decks, **Strength** is depicted as female, symbolic of the patience it takes to "tame a lion"; and the gentle, enduring qualities of the "perfect" woman, the **Strength** card represents that the virtue of Strength is not necessarily and aggressive male physical quality, but rather a gentle/passive, female one.

The **HERMIT** – Okay, we're settled in, have a mate, maybe a career – what about knowledge? By the time in our lives that the Hermit card would come up for us it would reflect either our desire for higher education; OR, that we have learned/experienced a great deal out of life and wish to share that

knowledge with others- - so, it is a student in search of learning; or it is a teacher in search of students wishing to acquire higher awareness of Life through taking advantage of someone else's experiences and using that shared knowledge to progress through Life more rapidly.

The **WHEEL OF FORTUNE** – Personal success and opportunity, when this card is upright- - also, acknowledgement that our positions in life are often tenuous; our rise to fame and fortune can easily be followed by a drop to anonymity; our successes forgotten or nullified, by one act of stupidity or simply a twist of fate. Because the **Wheel of Fortune** is round, it indicates that our path in life may be circular.

We start at some point on wheel- - certainly rarely at the top, and I believe we all start at different places on that wheel. Some of us are on the downward path- - those who were not born with advantages; others start at the bottom entirely and have nowhere else to go but up- - the key to the **Wheel of Fortune**, is to find our position, our place on the Wheel in the present and to see which way is UP... and then to proceed there. Also, to know when we've made it to the top of the Wheel- - how to MAINTAIN our position and guard against being unseated or led off to have to begin to traverse that Wheel again- - also, if one is very quick to catch on when they have been "de-throned" by other people or environmental circumstances- - take a close look at the spokes of the Wheel- - sometimes we may be able to take short-cuts to get back to the top.

The **Wheel of Fortune** is materialistic representation of competitiveness in humanity and the concept that in order for one to achieve, another must give up his/her place. It is not a card of cooperation or joint effort- - in a modern sense, it can depict the need to keep up with the materialistic standards and acquisitions of others…which is a never-ending circle both financially and socially.

JUSTICE – Right-Side up, this is Fairness in all things; Clear vision in decision making. Literally, it would represent a legal matter pending which will go well for you. Reverse, it is clouded vision, prejudice and someone who knows the difference between right and wrong, and is deliberately headed for the wrong side or the wrong choice.

The SACRIFICE - Religiously speaking, this represents Christ, the voluntary sacrifice of Christ for the salvation of mankind. Symbolically speaking, it is the representation of self-sacrifice- - usually occurring in relationships, marriages or family situations…sometimes in caring occupations, medical, (hospice); social/religious, such as missionary work; representing the highest good in the best of us.

DEATH – This card is controversial. It's number 13 in the Tarot deck; considered unlucky- -the symbolism is unclear. In Tarot, the card images for Death, is shown as the Grim Reaper, an animated skeleton coming to collect earth-bound beings; and other gruesome images, depending on the specific Tarot Deck. While many consider this card to represent major change and transition, which is a reasonable interpretation, it also, literally, is a reminder of Mortality. It's a half-way mark in our lives, which when it appears in a reading, reminds us to get closure; completion of our goals and desires- - it's like looking at a clock mid-way through our workdays and realizing the toughest part of the day is past…and we can look forward to going home.

TEMPERANCE – The patience to see something through to its logical conclusion. Understanding that just because we want something to happen as soon as we think of it, the Universe has its own order and it is the acceptance that all things happen in their own good time. Acceptance of timing in this Life is one of the most difficult lessons we need to learn. Our response is often instantaneous to situations; impulsive--sometimes that works out all right, but more often it is important to adopt the "wait and see" attitude that puts you more in synch with the way the Universe works. Temperance card reflects the use of logic and patience rather than emotion.

The DEVIL – Temptations along the way of Life. Usually physical in nature, but it can also be the need to have and acquire material things; the tendency toward treating people as possessions. The **Devil** in traditional religion was the Tempter who deceived Eve and encouraged Christ to renounce his Father and His purpose in exchange for the treasures of the physical world. This card literally represents being trapped and limited by our ties to material things- -"treasures" which can be taken away from us- -or even if we are allowed to acquire more than we can possibly need in one lifetime- -are still destined to

become useless as they cannot outlast what we are made of. It is best to define the things of the physical world AS temporary physical tools or toys and not define OURSELVES by how many of them we can acquire.

The **TOWER** – One of my favorites, the tower is another hint that we are becoming complacent in our lives- -just when we start taking what we have for granted, along comes a force of nature; another person or a new Thought or belief which so changes our lifestyle or our perspective on Life that we literally must choose other directions to go in because where we were or what we believed to be true, no longer applies- -we are forced to expand our horizons, usually because we wouldn't move an inch otherwise, if left to our own choice. Usually the over-conservative draw this card when it is their time for personal growth and forward momentum- --the Universe or Higher Power gives them a push... hopefully it is a gentle nudge rather than of hurricane force.

The **STAR** – Optimism; dreams finally starting to manifest into reality. This is a reward for patience and an acknowledgement of self-worth and value. It represents also, recognition from others for efforts you've made and usually represents appreciation that will be forthcoming by those around you. Great card for self-awareness and not minding having to stand alone, this card represents a person of great vision. Recognition of self as having a divine "light" within.

The **MOON** – Fear of the unknown and mystery are represented in the imagery of this card. Our fears either hold us back, or propel us forward at great speed. The true course of Life is Experience; and since there are no guarantees and many risks, the path beyond Fear and Risk leads to...

The **SUN** - ...rebirth; new beginnings, new thoughts and feelings. A putting of the past behind one as though reborn with regrets and guilt totally behind one.

JUDGEMENT – If **Death** is a half-time reminder, The card for **Judgement** is or can be physical death and the choices we are given at that moment of transition...to remain with our families as earth-bound spiritual beings; or to go on to the next level of our evolution, which is represented by:

The **WORLD** – The culmination of our Journey. The ability to look at the physical "world" or reality from a distance- -and that distance, depending on our religious beliefs, can be "heaven", or be part of the "Universal Life Force or the "Lifestream"...or to remain as an individual, cognizant entity, free-floating in another dimension...whatever that belief- -if we look at the progression from The Sun (Enlightenment, new birth) coming toward the end of a long and eventful life; we transcend the physical body with the **Judgement** card and we are given choices in the card of the **World,** as to whether or not we want to return to the limitations of the physical world we have just left, or to remain in the "spirit" entity form as part of a larger, meta-physical Universe. An Unseen world is not necessarily an ineffectual, non-influential one; nor is it necessarily one to be feared.

You must form your own opinions and interpretations of the symbolism pertaining to your particular, individual Tarot decks. This is just one set of definitions from which you may find many other interpretations based on your individual frame of references and experiences with Life. ALL Tarot cards are interpretive, and extremely diverse- -as diverse as the way each one of you sees and interacts with Life and the realities you are given to deal with during our journey through it.

Personal Opinions/Comments regarding Author's interpretation of The Life Journey as seen through the sequential Order of the Major Arcana:

_____

_____

_____

_____

_____

_____

_____

_____

_____

_____

_____

_____

_____

_____

_____

_____

_____

_____

_____

The Minor Arcana

*The important thing to remember about the **Minor Arcana** is that the **symbolism** on each of these cards serves the Reader in seeing the influences, people, situations and circumstances, both positive and negative, surrounding their client. <u>According to this author</u>,* the suits represent the following: **Swords** – conflict, difficulty, strength, endurance, the need for fortitude, but also, when the card shows a "person" holding a sword, that can represent that the person has the strength to overcome whatever obstacles are placed in front of them; they have survival skills- -and if there is no "person" in the card, just images of swords- -the right side up card represents a situation of influence surrounding your client in which they will very likely win over the opposition; and succeed in whatever their personal plan is--as long as they are willing to DO what it takes to get there.

Wands, Staffs, Staves, or Rods, represent the wispy things in life--spirituality, intellectual abilities, also on a practical level--Journey, Distance, Travel, mental philosophies, ideals and idealism.

Pentacles, in some decks they are called Disks or Starts- -this suit represented things of the physical, material world- -homes, money, job opportunities or disappointments, financial gain or loss.

Cups- the best suit in the deck and the one *which when absent* in someone's reading is a clear indication that they are not happy; that situations around them need to change, or that they need to take a closer look at their lifestyle or their present relationship(s) and make sure they are getting at least as good as they're giving.

Cups --The minor arcana cup cards are representative of things of the emotional world- -love, discouragement, disappointment, happiness, unhappiness, engagement, marriage, celebration between two friends, etc…if there's an emotion to be felt, it will be presented in a Cup card.

In Tarot Readings, most often for women, and occasionally for men, it is not unusual to find one partner in a marriage or other relationship, doing and giving their all, and the other partner is almost passive in their position in the relationship. Such an imbalance WILL appear in your Readings. We will work on Ethics and how to deliver possibly negative information, in another section. For now, the Minor Arcana Cup cards represent how we feel, how people around us feel and emotional situations headed our way.

Feel free to e-mail me with questions: a_maid55@yahoo.com. ***You must use your own individual Tarot Deck*** <u>to make your</u> **Minor Arcana** <u>meaningful to You, the Reader,</u> *based on your abilities to discern meanings from symbolic imagery.* (the information from pictures on the cards).

Notes on Ace of Wands:

_____

_____

_____

_____

Notes on 2 of Wands:

_____

_____

_____

_____

Notes on 3 of Wands:

_____

_____

_____

_____

Notes on 4 of Wands:

_____

_____

_____

_____

Notes on 5 of Wands:

_____

_____

_____

_____

Notes on 6 of Wands:

_____

_____

_____

_____

Notes on 7 of Wands:

_____

_____

_____

_____

Notes on 8 of Wands:

_____

_____

_____

_____

Notes on 9 of Wands:

_____

_____

_____

_____

Notes on 10 of Wands:

_____

_____

_____

_____

Notes on Prince OR page of Wands:

_____

_____

_____

_____

Notes on Princess of Wands:

_____

_____

_____

_____

Notes on Queen of Wands:

_____

_____

_____

_____

Notes on King of Wands:

_____

_____

_____

_____

Notes on Ace of Pentacles:

_____

_____

_____

_____

Notes on 2 of Pentacles:

_____

_____

_____

_____

Notes on 3 of Pentacles:

_____

_____

_____

_____

Notes on 4 of Pentacles:

_____

_____

_____

_____

Notes on 5 of Pentacles:

_____

_____

_____

_____

Notes on 6 of Pentacles:

_____

_____

_____

_____

Notes on 7 of Pentacles:

_____

_____

_____

_____

Notes on 8 of Pentacles:

_____

_____

_____

_____

Notes on 9 of Pentacles:

_____

_____

_____

_____

Notes on 10 of Pentacles:

_____

_____

_____

_____

Notes on Prince or Page of Pentacles:

_____

_____

_____

_____

Notes on Princess of Pentacles:

_____

_____

_____

_____

Notes on Queen of Pentacles:

_____

_____

_____

_____

Notes on King of Pentacles:

_____

_____

_____

_____

Notes on Ace of Swords:

_____

_____

_____

_____

Notes on 2 of Swords:

_____

_____

_____

_____

Notes on 3 of Swords:

_____

_____

_____

_____

Notes on 4 of Swords:

_____

_____

_____

_____

Notes on 5 of Swords:

_____

_____

_____

_____

Notes on 6 of Swords:

_____

_____

_____

_____

Notes on 7 of Swords:

_____

_____

_____

_____

Notes on 8 of Swords:

_____

_____

_____

_____

Notes on 9 of Swords:

_____

_____

_____

_____

Notes on 10 of Swords:

_____

_____

_____

_____

Notes on Prince or Page of Swords:

_____

_____

_____

_____

Notes on Princess of Swords:

_____

_____

_____

_____

Notes on Queen of Swords:

_____

_____

_____

_____

Notes on King of Swords:

_____

_____

_____

_____

Notes on Ace of Cups:

_____

_____

_____

_____

Notes on 2 of Cups:

_____

_____

_____

_____

Notes on 3 of Cups:

_____

_____

_____

_____

Notes on 4 of Cups:

_____

_____

_____

_____

Notes on 5 of Cups:

_____

_____

_____

_____

Notes on 6 of Cups:

_____

_____

_____

_____

Notes on 7 of Cups:

_____

_____

_____

_____

Notes on 8 of Cups:

_____

_____

_____

_____

Notes on 9 of Cups:

_____

_____

_____

_____

Notes on 10 of Cups:

_____

_____

_____

_____

Notes on Prince or Page of Cups:

_____

_____

_____

_____

Notes on Princess of Cups:

_____

_____

_____

_____

Notes on Queen of Cups:

_____

_____

_____

_____

Notes on King of Cups:

_____

_____

_____

_____

Sample Tarot Card Reading for Jesus Christ

The following Reading was generated by "random chance" from a very basic "entertainment" Tarot computer-software program. The selection of Jesus Christ for this exercise is specifically for the reason that he is the one figure that is universally recognized and familiar by Americans and others living in the USA, and that was the reason for the selection. We learn by comparisons and by calling on our experience and knowledge gained through study/education. It was felt that by selecting Jesus Christ, the process of Tarot Card Interpretation would be made clear, very quickly and through a readily identifiable subject/client. **The Author selected only the Significator (1st card) because of the limitations of the computer program.**

1. *Significator* – the client/oneself (The instructor selected **"The Hanged Man"**, Number 12 in the Major Arcana-- but called "The Sacrifice" in this workbook's Major Arcana examples..

The following were Computer selected "random" cards:

2. *This Crosses one- Obstacles and opposing forces regarding client's present position.*

KNIGHT OF WANDS: An attractive man who lives life in the fast lane; a risk taker and an idealistic dreamer; wands this may also symbolize sudden change, journey, distance, travel...

3. *This is beneath one,* The foundation and history of the present matter...

FIVE OF WANDS Success does not bring satisfaction- -and too much desire and striving ultimately leads to loss.

4. *This is Behind One-* Influences that remain from the past.

FOUR OF WANDS – Bountiful Harvest; inspiration, devotion to duty hoping to bring unification of purpose to share that bountiful harvest.

5. *This is Above one.*

DEATH- This card predicts enormous and possibly traumatic changes. The end of an era leads to new experiences, rebirth, despair giving way to hope and so on. Next to a Court card it means that the change will come through the person symbolized. Near future—4 weeks.

(NOTE: A Court card is a king, queen, prince, page, or princess etc...)

6. *This card is before/ahead of one*

FIVE OF PENTACLES –Misery loves company; suffering; false friend; greed.

7. *This is oneself, back in the present.* What to expect in the days to come.

KNIGHT OF PENTACLES- A well-read man who may work as an educator and explores knowledge, moreso than life's comforts and pleasures. Wealth is of no interest to him, as the Universe provides all his needs, through Faith.

8. *This represents ones family, friends, social environment or work.* in the present.

SEVEN OF SWORDS- Through hard labors, a wish will come true.

9. *This card's position represents <u>Hopes and Fears</u>—but not necessarily the present reality.*

SIX OF WANDS- Good news, success, the fulfillment of long-awaited desires. A gathering together of friends of like minds. **OR**, Disappointment ahead; deception and betrayal affecting not only the client, but others who follow his lead.

10. *The most important Card position: Far future/ Final Outcome* (within a year)

Future outcome based on *present path progression,* and influences of other cards.

TEN OF SWORDS--Success will not be enough to avoid the pain and misery that will come. TheTen of Swords is possibly the most visually negative card in the minor arcana—a body with ten swords sticking straight up out of it—not Death—but possibly being so much in physical and/or mental distress that one couldn't be blamed for *wishing* for Death—how accurate might that card's forecast be during what historical religious doctrine tells us about Christ's last few moments before His ultimate Sacrifice?

Although there are only ten cards in most Celtic Cross Layouts, I have always taken at leat one—sometimes as many as four cards in a Progression on that Far Future card to get a little more information. The extra card drawn for the reading for Jesus Christ was very enlightening:

ACE OF CUPS -- Love, compassion, generosity and kindness will lead to future success, and a good public image.

A more optimistic ending than the accurate, but somewhat premature destiny of the traditional 10-card Celtic Cross. Never hesitate to "extend" your Reading to end with hope rather than disappointment or failure. It's ALL in the Cards.

Tarot Reader's Notes or Comments:

_____

_____

_____

_____

_____

_____

_____

_____

Opinion: Agree or Disagree with the Following:

The Major Arcana is thought to be the definitive Journey through Life from birth (awareness) to death (transformation/transition to another plane of existence; an afterlife)

_____

_____

_____

_____

_____

OR:

The Major Arcana is a GUIDELINE or Blueprint, which when followed in order, is the quickest way to personal fulfillment of Divine Purpose of Plan...although other paths may still lead one to personal success and the fulfillment of Divine Purpose or Plan...albeit with many "side trips" which are camouflaged as "bad" choices or "mistakes" or "errors in judgement".

_____

_____

_____

_____

_____

OR:

Your own interpretation of the purpose of the Tarot's Symbolism

_____

_____

_____

_____

<u>*If you would like a free critique you may mail this page to me at:*</u>

Lady Anne

P.O. Box 12

Connelly Springs, NC 28612

I hope you enjoyed this workbook and it is useful to you on your path of self-empowerment, enlightenment and your personal road to happiness and success.

www.ingramcontent.com/pod-product-compliance
Lightning Source LLC
Chambersburg PA
CBHW041131280526
45792CB00013B/2380